BOOK NAME: Toddlers' animals coloring books for beginners grade 1 to 6

WRITER NAME: Muhammad Waqar Ul Hassan

This book is for knowledge and study purpose.

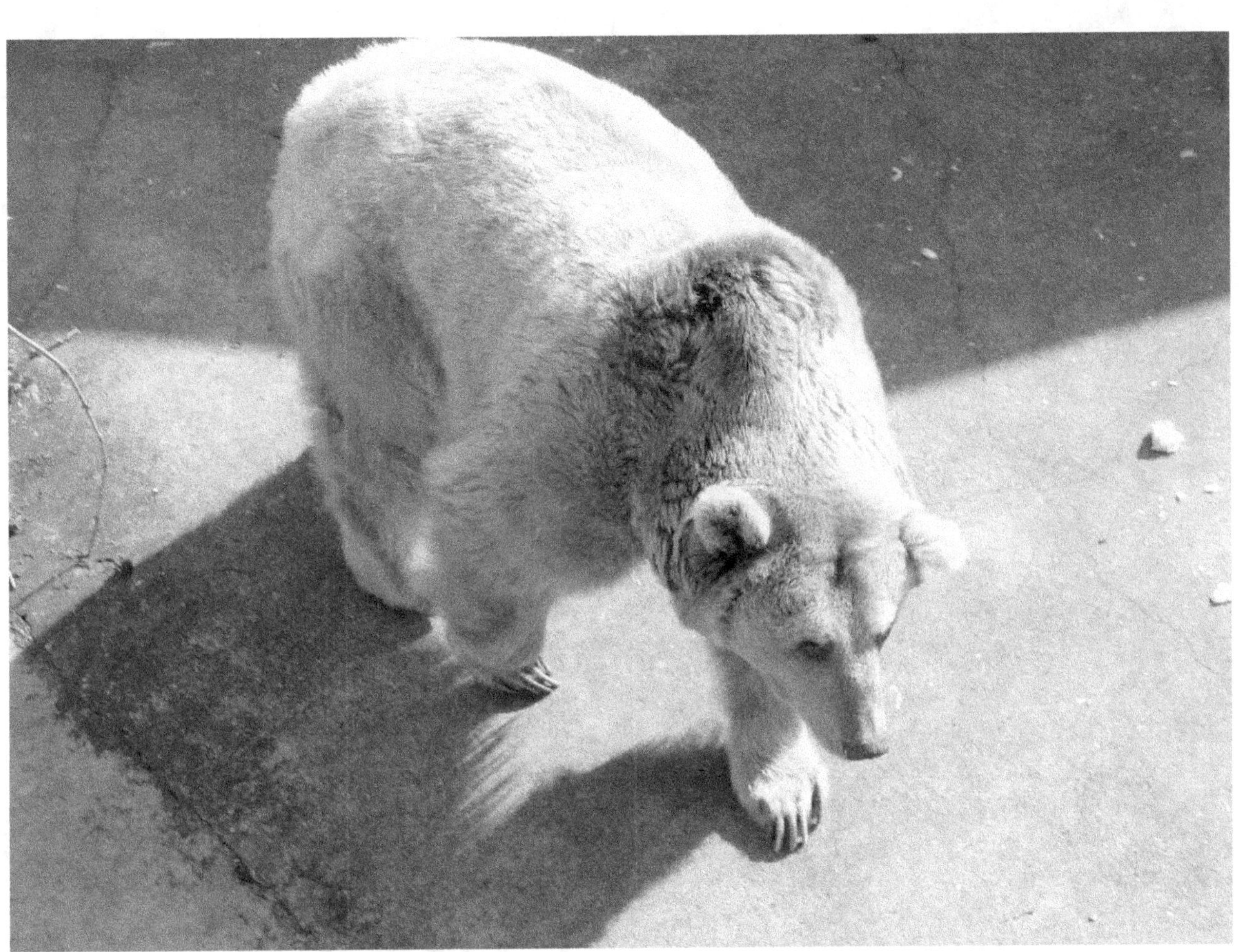

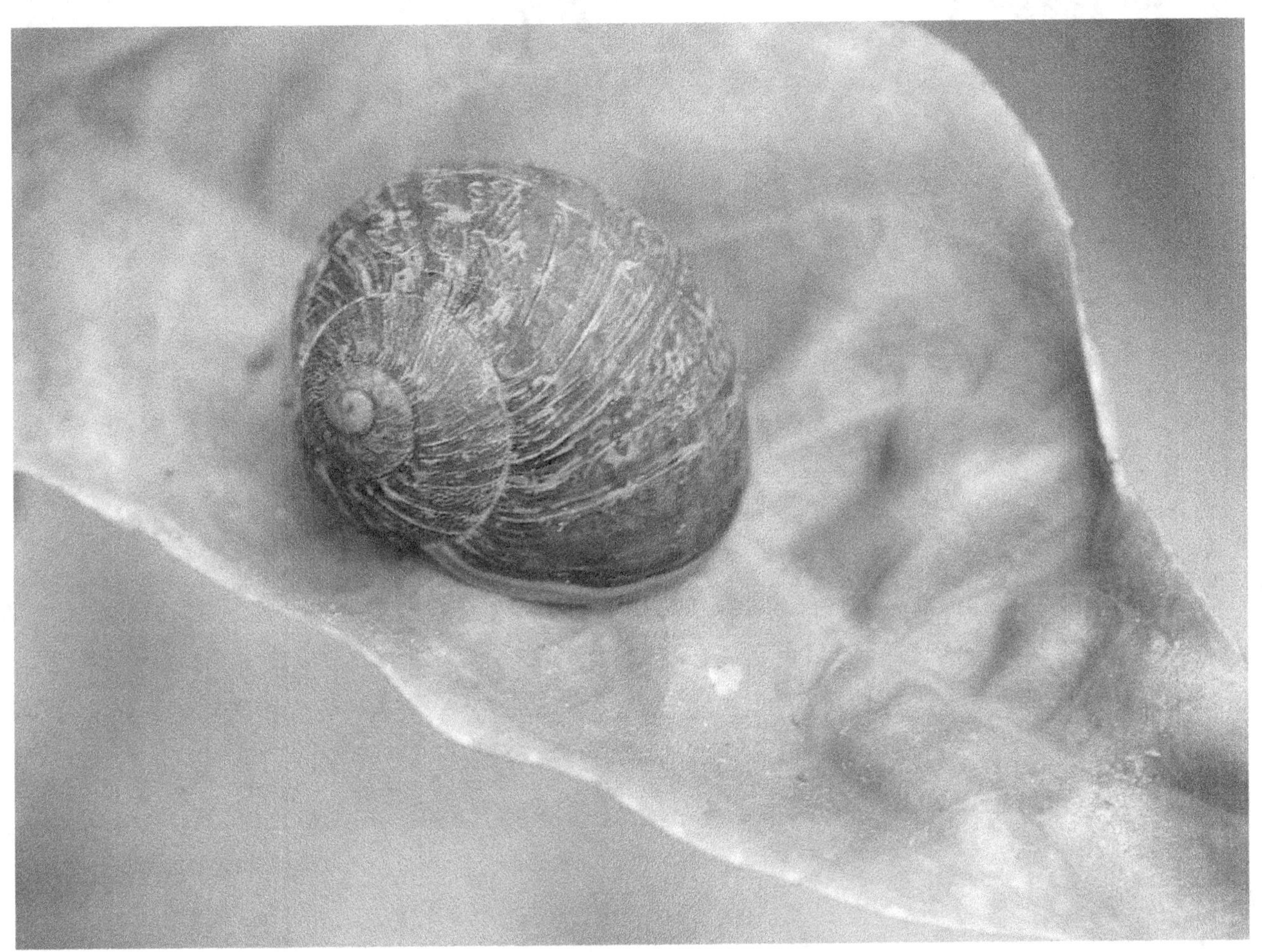

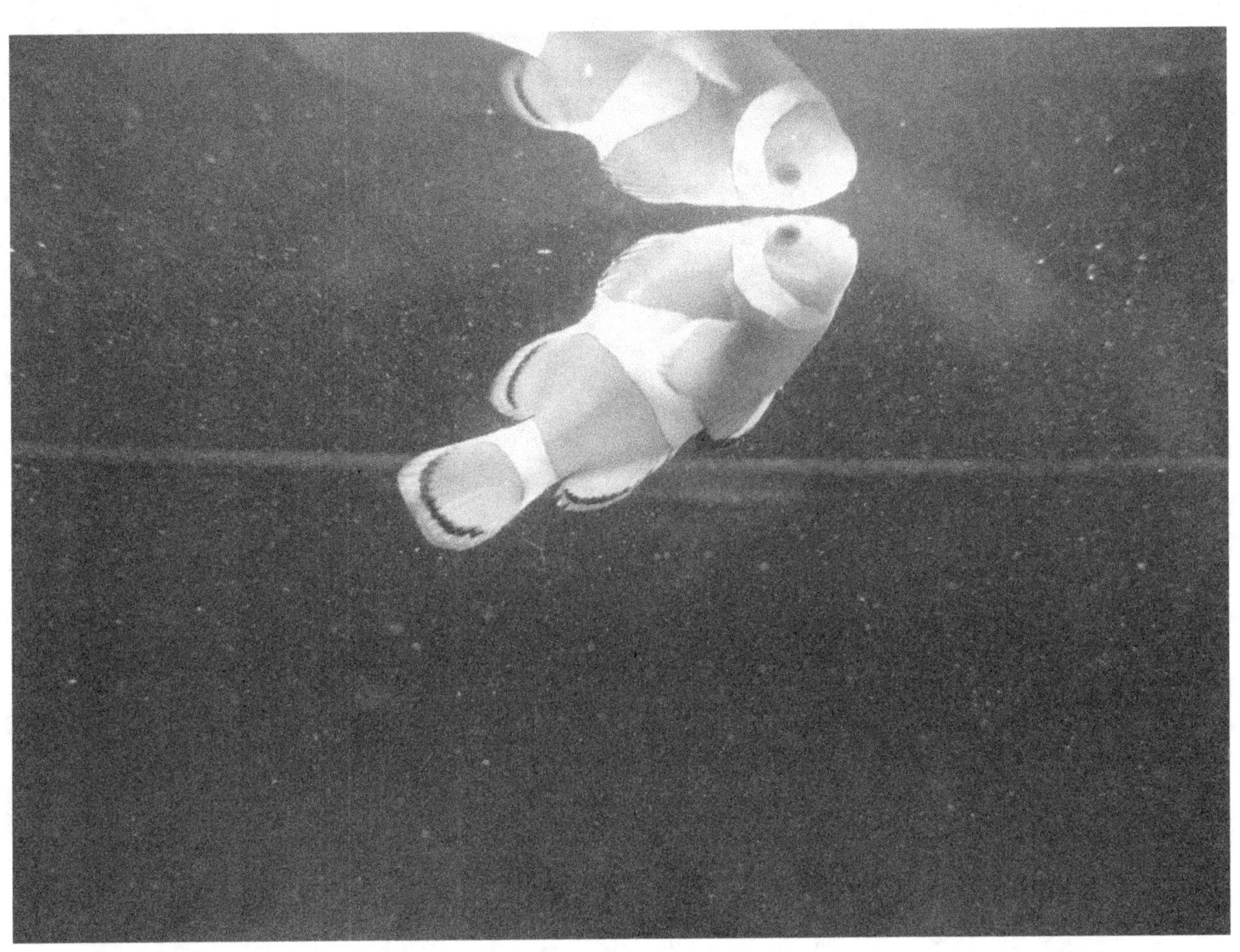

www.ingramcontent.com/pod-product-compliance
Lightning Source LLC
Chambersburg PA
CBHW080729120726
48001CB00010B/3176